MY INVISIBLE INJURY

Living Life with a Traumatic Brain Injury

Written By: Katie L. Patterson

 www.trafford.com

North America & international
toll-free: 1 888 232 4444 (USA & Canada)
phone: 250 383 6864 ♦ fax: 812 355 4082

Contents

About the Author:

Katie L. Patterson known by all of her friends and family as Kate is a happy and intelligent 25-year-old young woman. She participates in wheelchair tennis and adaptive water skiing, when the weather is appropriate. Excelling in college, studying Nursing she holds honors. She is a great friend and wonderful daughter and she has a HUGE Heart. Kate has a disability, but she doesn't consider herself disabled (except for the parking benefit).

In this book, you will read some of the extreme challenges she endured.

Before you flip to the next page and start your journey through my accident. Please, if you know anyone who rides a bike or motorcycle, skateboards or long boards, rollerblades or anything like that. Make sure they wear a helmet and buckle their seatbelts. I promise, you will never regret wearing a helmet or buckling that seatbelt! It will save your life!

1
April 22ⁿᵈ 2008

It was a beautiful day, the smell of fresh cut grass filled the air and the sun was shining so bright. It was the first time in days, in which it hadn't rained. The streets were finally dry, a perfect day! I needed a one-day break, from life. I wish I would have known then, what I know now. That one-day off has turned into almost three years. But, I had grown up so quickly. I had already served for the United States Army as a 92M. I was now working full time as a nanny and studying nursing at J. Sargent Reynolds community college. At the age of 20, I had purchased my first home! It was gorgeous! Gorgeous green siding with red window shutters, it was 1600 sqft with 3 bedrooms and 2 bathrooms.

No one I knew that was my age; had done that; everyone was partying and living life. Not worrying about carpeting their home or tiling their backsplash, into a sorority or a fraternity. Simply hoping that they wouldn't get caught for underage drinking. They were living the life of a typical 20 year old. But, I was no typical 20 year old. I felt like I was extremely mature for my age, doing things that people twice my age hadn't done before. I was stepping into a commitment, by signing the loan agreement to turn the key into my new home.

Being in college was amazing! I had made a wonderful friend, Cherise. We were in Anatomy and Physiology together, which was taught by whom I consider to be the best teacher of all times, her name, was Dr. Oteilla Vines. There were some classes I could not stand in college, i.e. math. But, anatomy and physiology was a class that I loved! Cherise and I took frequent smoke breaks together and also built a wonderful friendship together. It was nice, being able to find time to do things with friends. It kind of gave me a break, from trying to manage being a full time student, a full time employee, and a homeowner.

It had been raining all week and the previous weekend. I hated when it rained. I couldn't longboard through the hills of my neighborhood or sit on my back porch and enjoy the sunshine. It wasn't raining on Tuesday April 22nd, 2008, for the first time in days! I made a decision, now that I regret! I called in sick to work, which is something I didn't often do. But, I just needed a day of freedom. A day where there wasn't a worry in the world.

My neighbor David had been joking around, daring me to longboard down his very steep driveway. I knew I could do it; I had faith in my longboarding abilities. The roads were dry, for the first time in days. I couldn't wait to feel the vibration of the wheels against the textures of the concrete and the wind blowing softly through my curly hair. I prepared to go down the driveway. I had my left foot on that board, with my right foot prepared to push off.

Off off and away… I pushed myself quickly and fiercely. Down the driveway, moving smoothly. Feeling the wind blowing through my hair. It was amazing, pushing off with my right foot, only to get a faster speed and faster as I continued down the steep incline. Until, Ruetker and Lucas came running down the road. Ruetker went to grab his board, so he could join me, but Lucas stood right in my path. I was moving so quickly, with no way to avoid him. I screamed fiercely for him to move, but he didn't. In a quick worried choice, I jumped off of my board.

This is what I have been told through ambulance reports, phone calls, and eyewitness reports. I have been told that I was very mean and violent towards the EMT and ambulance drivers. I was hitting and biting them. I kept saying, "Nothing is wrong with me!" In that moment, no one had any idea in how badly injured I was. People just assumed I had fractured my leg. However, I was severely injured, without a clue! By the time I made it to the hospital at MCV Medical Center, I was critical. I had major injuries to my skull and brain, as well as a severe tibial platue fracture to my left leg. There was an extreme amount of pressure and swelling in my brain. At that point, both injuries were severe, not one worse than the other.

The next part has been copied from a friend's blog posting, who was there during the whole entire first few days of my injury!

Katie has a bleeding artery in her brain, a broken temporal bone, a broken frontal bone, and a contusion to the occipital lobe of her brain. Her left leg is so severe that it is just as important as her brain trauma. As of today (Thursday) April, 24th she has had one of several surgeries needed for her leg, the bleeding in her brain has continued (but not worsened), and she finally was able to breathe on her own today. Her parents flew out on Wednesday morning to be with her.

Katie is out of it and has no idea what's going on. None of us have had a real conversation with her, because she is messed up right now. She does know who her Mom and Dad are. She will say their names when she hears their voices.

It is horrific when she actually wakes up for a minute or two, because she is so violent and out of it due to the head trauma in combination with high levels of pain pills. She has several contusion on her brain and that can really alter a persons actions and thought process.

Her parent's have been by her side every day. Last night, she had a seizure and it now looks as if the brain swelling is back. They are not able to dilate both pupils at the current time.

Due to the fact that she is in the neuroscience intensive care unit, the visiting hours are very limited and only immediate family can come in. We are all praying for her and know she'll get through this. Kate's a tough gal, so we know she'll be okay in time.

The doctors are saying it will be a very long recovery and she won't be able to leave the hospital for months.

So, all of that was happening and I was completely in and out of it! Some days I was completely blind and other days I could distinguish colors and light. My health was a constant battle; I was fighting diligently for my life. I was having seizures, which caused more swelling in my brain. Some days were better than others, at times I was healing and at times my health was getting worse.

By April 29th, it had been seven days since I had anything to eat; I finally had my first bite of food. I ate a small amount of fruit. I was also finally off of life support. I was breathing more on my own and was becoming more and more stable as each day passed. MCV Hospital was hoping to get me out of their intensive care and into a regular unit, where I would still receive 24-hour care. The speech therapist came in today and did and evaluation to explain and measure the severity of my brain injury! On a scale of 1 to 10, ten being the highest level of brain function: I was a level 3. My hospital stay continued and it would need to for months and months. But, almost three years later my recovery and healing is still happening.

I wasn't allowed to have many visitors, because I was in the intensive care unit. But, my good friend and ex-roommate was able to stop by, Kyra who was able to get in and see me. "I saw Kate smile for the first time when I said, "Kate - look! It's Kyra Beaver" She looked in Kyra's direction, smiled and waved." However, my Mom, Dad, Aunt Bonnie, Sister and Brother rotated time spent with me in the hospital. My Mom never left my side, she used the family medical leave option associated with her job and dedicated those months to ensuring that I was being taken care of. My father was there as often as he could be, as was my brother and sister. My Aunt Bonnie was a fundamental part of my Mom's strength. My Mom was fighting battles for my health every single day. Luckily my wonderful and caring family was able to help. Taking turns in coming to Virginia to play a vital roll in my recovery and in my Mom's strength.

I was still being treated at MCV Hospital, in Richmond Virginia at this point. However, my Mom was working diligently with the staff at Richard L. Roudebush VA Medical Center in Indianapolis, Indiana to get me transferred. There are very few Brain Trauma hospitals across the nation; we were lucky to find one in our home state of Indianapolis, Indiana.

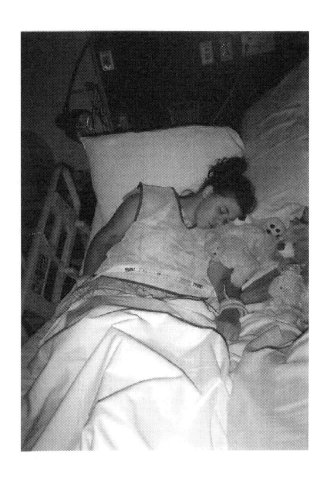

2
The OK has been given

I was finally given clearance to fly home, to Indiana. My family hired a flight nurse to accompany me home. I was picked up by an ambulance from MCV and was taken to the airport. The flight was terrible! We didn't have a private chartered plain or a helicopter. We took a normal flight! I had an external fixator attached to my left leg and people were bumping into it. However, a flight nurse did accompany my Mom and me on the flight from Richmond, VA to Atlanta, GA and from Atlanta to our final stop to Indianapolis, IN.

In my Mom's words:

> OMG - We are home - the trip on the plane was a tough one, but we made it. The tears started flowing from Atlanta to Indy - I was so overwhelmed with joy to be going home, and taking my daughter to a hospital where she will be cared for appropriately. Without my sisters help in Virginia, I would have fallen apart. We fought so many battles for Katie's care. The last 12 days at the Richmond Hospital were pretty much nil in her care. It was like she was at a hotel, with a sitter, meds and that is basically it. Bonnie and I washed her, combed her hair, walked with her, gave her physical therapy, changed her sheets daily, etc. It saddens me that the medical industry would take an oath and not follow thru.

> When we arrived at the VA hospital, there were many people introducing themselves, and reassuring

me that Katie would be taken care of. The nursing staff cried with me. She is now receiving top-notch care! She receives PT, OT, Recreational Therapy, Speech Therapy and they are coming twice per day. The physician, Dr. Andrew Mosier, is awesome - he jumped for joy knowing he was receiving Katie on his PolyTrauma Unit – the unit had just opened and Katie is their first patient. She is the only female in the hospital and most patients are over the age of 65. They are thrilled they have a patient who they can measure improvements from. I cannot express to you the joy I feel at this present moment.

The first thing they did was take her off of Haldol, which kept her drugged for 22 days. They all were so upset to know she was on this horrible drug. She actually laughed today - the first sign of emotion she has had. I cry thinking of this small sign of improvement.

She sang songs to all of the staff members today - "Jesus take the wheel" and apologized to all for not singing well. She is improving so much. Surgery for her leg most likely will take place next week. Thank for your support, prayers and your donations. I shall never forget the kindness that I have received.

Thank you Terry - KT's Mom

I can't even imagine the emotions that my Mom had! We have discussed my accident a few times, since I came to. The tears that flow fiercely down her face when the conversation gets intense is scary. I wouldn't have known how to handle the situation, had I been in her shoes! You never want to see your parents cry, but I know for so long she has held back so many emotions. I think for a long time, she didn't think I could hear about the severity of my injury. She felt that she was protecting me, by keeping certain instances private. But, finally we have had that talk. We have sat down and talked for hours, discussing those scary months. It was amazing to hear about my accident, coming from her. Because, my accident is still a complete mystery to me, I feel like no matter how much I hear about it, I will never understand it.

It's amazing the wonderful nurses, physical therapists, and staff at the Richard L. Roudebush VAMC. I was on the road to recovery. Sandi and Tashia were my two favorite day nurses. Typically one of those two ladies was in my room with me, as I needed 24 hour care. I had a funny way of associating things, so that I could remember their names. I called Tashia, Tasheeea and Sandi was always referred to as Sandi Pandolli, which is her full name. They were incredible and wonderful women. I also had a few other nurses, but I can't remember their names. Which frustrates me, but that's part of my brain injury. Forgetfulness. I am so thankful that there were so many loving people, who opened their hearts to treating me and to ensure that I would get the best health care possible. I realize that they take an oath and it is there duty and obligation to care for the patients in their units and on their floors. But, that doesn't always happen. To some people being a nurse is just another job, but to good nurses it is there life. They know, that sometimes those patients and their families need a strong support staff and they did there do diligence to ensure that my family felt welcomed and at peace, knowing I was finally getting the healthcare and treatment that I needed. Also, I can't ever forget my social worker, the women who made the bed available. I know that without Robbie's help, this wouldn't have happened as smoothly as it did. So, thanks Robbie!

I will never remember my time in the hospital in full, but I remember bits and pieces of my extended stay in there. I have no memory of my accident and I probably never will. I think that God does that to protect us. He doesn't want us to suffer through those terrible times over and over again in our heads. I know that I was very sick and close to death, but I can't remember the extreme pain I was in. But, I do remember a few small details of being in the hospital. The things that I remember from my hospitalization are my sassy attitude and loving spirit. I connected in so many ways with so many of my caretakers.

Again I am copying some more information from the Blog that was started by my family, so people could watch my progress and continue warm thoughts and prayers towards my recovery and prayers for strength for my family.

Wow, KT is amazing! She is hopping around like a champ. Her attitude is amazing. I absolutely love being with her - she makes me smile. She keeps telling me how happy she is to be in Indy as she has missed her family terribly. She knows she has had an accident now and gets frustrated because she can't remember things -I keep telling her "I will be your memory", and she apologizes for that.

She jokes with the staff, and they joke back with her. They told me yesterday that they are looking for a discharge of July 11th - 6 weeks away as a target date. She will need 24 hour care for one year -----They are looking for a day program for her to stimulate her mind, and receive the therapies she will need. She knows I need to go back to work in a week, and she understands that I have to, but tells me how much she will miss me.

I know God has a plan for us through this experience. So many good things have happened as a result of this horrible injury. I had no idea how much love our family and friends would give. It gives me chills to think of all of the kindness I have received. I will give it back - "pay it forward" ---- I have learned so much about brain injuries ----and the feelings a family goes through with all of it.

The Daily Journal is doing a story on KT and it will be ran the week prior to her 5K run/walk - the article will focus her story and the importance of helmets and safety.

Thank you again to all of our family and friends. When I tell Kt what the community is doing, she cries -------- Terry KT's Mom

God does have a plan; sometimes we question why such terrible things happen to such wonderful people. But, it is all in His plan! I guess it's so one day, someone might hear about my accident and be able to relate. Maybe their son or daughter likes to skateboard or someone in their family has a traumatic brain injury.

Today was good. Had to get a birth certificate for KT for her Social Security application on Monday. She had her stitches taken out today - she cried - However, the sassy KT yelled at the doc removing them - that is so what KT would do. Her therapists are so impressed with her recovery, as am I. God is so good.

Sweet story: Michael is a veteran who has diabetic feet and is in a wheel-chair - I met Michael a few days after KT was admitted - he would be bumming cigarettes, and one day ask me if I could get him a diet coke. I told him to wheel himself to 4 West and I would give him KT's diet cokes. He did. A few days later, when I would see him, I ask him if he was a patient in the VA hospital. He said he was, but was sleeping at the Wheeler Mission at night, and wheeling himself back to the VA in the daytime as the Missions make you leave in the morning. He wheels himself about 2 miles back to the VA. My sister and I went to lunch one day and brought Michael lunch back. He wheeled himself to 4 west trying to pay us (which he has very little money), and we refused his dollars, and went about our business.

The nurse comes to the room yesterday with a planter and note from Michael - he bought my daughter a plant and wrote her a note - "Katie - get better soon - Michael ---------This sweet veteran with his garbage bag full of his belongings, in a wheelchair bought my daughter a planter - - how sweet is that!

"Pay it forward"

.........Kid, if that won't bring tears to your eyes, nothing will --

Paying it forward is so important. I don't ever remember meeting Michael and I don't remember seeing the flowers that he got for me, however, I feel touched by his generosity. The man was homeless, yet took the time and what little money he had, to buy me, who he didn't know some beautiful flowers. At times, even when we have very little taking a few minutes and helping someone else can be extremely beneficial. You never know someone's story, just by looking at him or her. However, sometimes you can see parts of their story, just by looking into their eyes! One of my Mom's favorite sayings is "Pay it forward!" She uses that quite regularly and it is so true. If one person has ever done a good deed for you, please pass on the love!

So, we are preparing for my discharge from the hospital. I was so scared. I was terrified of falling and I was also scared that I wouldn't get the interactions that I was getting inpatient. I had people in my room constantly at the VA. But, now that I was getting discharged, I was fearful of not being able to get out and about. Meet new friends, etc.

3
Home Sweet Home

KT is home - I took her to Steak n' Shake per her request -- she is tired, but so excited. Her nursing staff, doctors, and therapists were sad to see her go, yet happy for her. A number of them plan to visit. She went to see an ENT today and her hearing in her right ear is severe with a hearing loss - they fit her for a hearing aide, which will be ready to pick up in a few weeks -- she is totally ok with it. As we were driving home, and passed our old church, she indicated she is praying now, and wants to go back to church :) KT's Mom

I guess it had all hit me, that there was a reason I was still alive. I had no clue what that reason was, but I knew I needed faith to continue to push me through. God had saved me for some reason. I needed to praise Him!

I went to church that Sunday and felt very awkward. It had been a really long time since I had walked through those church doors. I saw a few familiar faces, but I didn't feel welcomed, I am sure that was because of my degraded self-image. I never went back to that church again. I felt so uncomfortable there.

On a lighter note: my amazing and loving cousin Lauren Patterson helped to put together a benefit walk/run to help raise money to pay for the cost of transporting me from Richmond, VA to Indianapolis, IN. It was called "Katie's Kause". So many people came to that event, people I didn't even know. Others donated money, so that I could be transferred to Indianapolis, Indiana. I feel so grateful, that people were willing to take time, from their busy schedules to walk in my honor, for my health. I am forever grateful for the kindness and good spirit of those who surrounded themselves around me. I feel blessed to have such close friends and a wonderful and caring family!

Also, a few dear and loyal friends made sure they were there for the event. Dawn flew all the way from Utah, to be there for the big event! It was a huge surprise. I knew that my friend Katie Marie B was going to be there, but she didn't ruin the surprise. I was so very excited to see Dawn. It was an amazing day, to be able to see how many people loved and cared about me. I am so blessed!

It was very successful, so many people showed their support! It was absolutely amazing!

WOW, what a huge success on Saturday for KT's Kause. There were 175 people I was told -- it was so organized and well ran. Lauren did an excellent job organizing this event along with her sister, coach and friends. The T-shirts were adorable! The weather totally cooperated - I was so worried about rain, but said a huge prayer and we were dry - God is so good -----

Thank you all who participated -- KT mentioned this morning, that she is so amazed at how kind people are and she is absolutely correct -- We are truly blessed to have friends and family who care so much!

Katie's Kause

June 28, 2008
5K Run or Walk Benefit

On April 22, 2008, Katie, a fun, loving person full of life, decided to have a little fun. She rode a skateboard down a hill and jumped off to avoid hitting a child. As a result, she suffered a brain injury and multiple leg fractures.

She was transferred to Indianapolis from Virginia where the accident occurred and is currently undergoing treatment to regain her memory and multiple surgeries for her leg.

Katie Patterson
Age: 22
Nursing Major

Katie's Kause was established to help Katie with her medical expenses and future rehabilitation of her injuries.

Family & friends have joined together to support Katie and you are invited to join us and learn how Katie touched the lives of others.

June 28, 2008

8:00 a.m. Registration
9:00 a.m. Run & Walk will begin

Province Park, Franklin
see back for more details

Thank you from the bottom of our hearts! I brought KT to work with me this am and a wheelchair company will pick her up and transport her to RHI on the North side for her therapies - she was up this am, made her bed, packed her lunch and she was ready to go - she is becoming very independent! Also, no pain pills for the last 3 days ------ She is healing quite nicely KT's MOM

So, I am home. My social worker and therapy team decided that I needed aggressive therapies. So, they sent me to a program through RHI, where I would see a Psychologist, Speech Therapist, Recreational Therapist, Vision Therapist, and Physical Therapist. At that point I still wasn't able to drive, so they hired a driver for me, his name was Bill! He was a very nice guy! We chitchatted on the way to therapy every day that he picked me up!

It's now September, 5 months in recovery from that terrifying day.

As most of you know, her accident was 4/22/08 -- She had a plateau fracture, and brain injury. We are now almost five months into this whole ordeal. She has approximately 14 medical providers whom she sees weekly and some monthly. As far as her leg, she is now walking with crutches - she is only allowed to put 20 lbs. of weight on her bad leg. The orthopedic surgeon indicated to us two weeks ago that her tibia is still broke. It is a long process. One day she will need a knee replacement, but obviously is way too young.

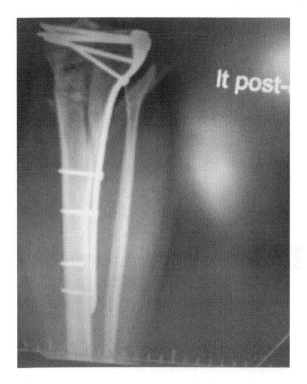

She was told she probably needed to rethink her career as she will never be able to weight bear all day for a job. Her goal to be a nurse is now being reconsidered.

She has therapy for her leg twice per week now. She sees the surgeon again on Sept 24th. As far as the brain injury, she lost her hearing in her right ear, and wears a hearing aide. She lost her vision on the left side of each eye, and now has glasses with prisms. She is trying to get use to them. She has severe headaches, in which she takes meds for and depression, in which she takes antidepressants for. Her life has turned inside out, and she is trying to adjust as all of us are. She wants to drive and be independent again, and I keep telling her she will get there in due time. It's all about healing and taking one day at a time. The medical maize we are currently in can be overwhelming.

As a Mom, I want to ensure she is taken care and taken to all of her appointments. I finally realized that I couldn't be super Mom, super wife, mother, caretaker, and an employee. Katie has a driver, Bill who helps me out significantly by picking her up and bringing her home.

On VA appointments, I try my hardest to take her, but our friend Ko Ko (our VA buddy) who is amazing helps me out with VA appointments. It's pretty crazy and we are all exhausted, yet thrilled that our Katie is progressing. She has a hard time realizing all of her progress because she has no memory of the accident, or most of the hospitalization and procedures; therefore, she gets anxious wanting things to move faster. Our family, friends have been awesome.

The prayers are the best for KT and we ask that you all continue to pray for a full recovery for her.

Recovery was a battle everyday. I can remember going to RHI and getting terrified of the smallest things! I can remember refusing to go on outings, because I thought I would get lost. I was terrified of being out in public without someone to watch over me. Speech therapy constantly reminded me of my brain injury. I would get so mad at myself, because I could see that I wasn't remembering things that I needed to remember. I cried a lot. I was disappointed in myself, for not being able to heal quickly. But, what I didn't know is that with a brain injury it takes time, a long time to heal and re-adjust to your new life.

And, ohhh, how I hated physical therapy and the daily exercises I had to do. It's not that I hated the idea of it, because that wasn't the case. I just hated the pain associated with the exercises. Riding a bike is supposed to be an easy thing; most kindergartners can do it with ease. But, riding on that stationary bike, feeling my leg grind as I pushed the petal felt like complete torture.

Everyday was like the first day of recovery from my injury. I had a really hard time realizing how far I had come. I was constantly getting angry with myself, assuming that I hadn't made any progress in my recovery. I felt like everyday was the same day as before, with nothing gained. I was so naïve.

There were so many amazing people at RHI. I remember the receptionist was extremely sweet. She seemed to not see my disabilities, yet saw my outgoing personality and she would talk to me everyday that I came in. Like I have said before, I don't remember many things, but Paula holds a place in my heart. Because, she didn't know me before my disability, but she connected with me, she didn't see my brain injury, she saw me. Also, Dr. Backhaus was incredibly sweet. Her job through RHI was to work with TBI patients and Stroke victims and to council them, to learn strategies relating to there new disabilities. She was a great therapist and was committed to being the best doctor possible. Then there was Connie my Physical therapist! I knew Connie before working with her at RHI, as she used to work with my Mom at Advanced Physical therapy! So it was nice, to see a familiar face. Then there was Beth, my speech therapist. Last but not least, I worked with Rosemary; she was my vision therapist and a very sweet lady. The staff at RHI was very kind and had open hearts. They were a vital part to my recovery and I am very thankful to the women who worked with me on that!

4
A small set back...

KT has done so well given the horrible accident. She has been quite a trooper. However, she has had a black slide. Over the weekend, she totally lost her vision out of her left eye. If she closes her right eye, everything is black. To make the situation worse, because she lost her left visual field, which means she has no vision from the mid point of her eye over to the left, therefore, she only has partial sight in her right eye. She sees very little.

She now can't drive -------------she bumps into things................she was signed up for school, and now can't see to drive or study.

Her sense of hearing is limited due to no hearing in her right ear, her sense of sight is limited more significantly now, and she has no sense of taste or smell. Three of her senses are limited! Please pray for KT as this has set her over the edge. She feels helpless. My heartaches for her right now! She had a brain scan last night; perhaps she has swelling in her brain, which is compromising her ocular nerve!
------No results yet KT's Mom

Every time I was doing better, it seemed that something else got worse. I was so frustrated. I just wanted to be like everyone else my age. I hated knowing that I was disabled.

I was sinking into a very deep depression. I kept asking myself, why is this happening to me? What have I done in my short life that has been so awful? I must have done something awful, as no good person can have such turmoil happen to him or her. That's the way I thought. Thinking back now, God never gives you more than you can handle.

I was supposed to start school, but this stopped me from moving forward. I tried to keep my spirits up and I did. I just continued to figure out my life. I was worried, though, because I was planning on going to school for graphic design. So, would I be able to still see well enough to accomplish those goals?

Looking back now, I can remember how confused and upset I was. I remember how hard those times were. Why were these things happening to me? I wanted so badly to be back in school and to try to continue with my educational goals. I needed to see my future progressing, instead of slipping into a hole. But, without being able to drive, I wasn't sure how I could do that. How could I continue to push myself? How could someone with severe vision loss be successful? I doubted myself everyday, I sometimes still struggle with this. But, I take a moment to look back and see the struggles that I have overcome and I get it. I start to realize that there is no reason that I shouldn't have faith in what will happen to me. I know that there is hope. I know that I will still be able to set goals and be able to reach them, I just have to remember that there are things that I cannot do, anymore. But, that doesn't mean I can't do anything.

5
It's Been 1 Year

It's been a year since that fateful day! Sure, my TBI has severely affected a few things, but one thing no one or no injury besides death will ever be able to change is my perseverance. I was to start school on the anniversary of my life.

I had to make some huge adjustments in my life. I didn't know that there were disability services at every university across the nation. I didn't know that they had note-takers to help students out. When I learned about the help I could get while I was in school, I was so excited. Because, I had doubts about being able to get my degree! However, once I learned that, I knew I would graduate from college!

I am sure a lot of people assume: it's been a year; nothing will get better! I extremely disagree with that. Please, don't give up hope!

I am thrilled to know that I will be able to start my life over again. I am changing my major, as my previous major is not possible now due to my disabilities. I was going to school to be a nurse pre my accident now I am going to study graphic design and a minor in digital photography. Luckily my TBI didn't affect my artist abilities.

Tomorrow will be one day since I fell on that fateful accident! You know I have grown a lot in this year! Who would have ever thought that when life hands you lemons your make a strong glass of lemonade. Many days I wish that I hadn't had this terrible accident because it has made life very hard for me! I am half blind, half deaf, can't taste or smell and my memory... well my memory is still terrible! I decided that I was ready to get back into school! I completely changed my major! I am now studying graphic design and photography at the Art Institute of Indy!

The following was something I had written in my own blog, to celebrate my year alive.

It is amazing. I am currently taking two classes Color Theory and Critical Thinking! I have had three leg surgeries and I have been told that I need two more. I will schedule those soon! I am still in physical therapy as well as speech therapy so that I can relearn ways to studying considering the fact that school is a lot harder for me now! I hope that I just get back to the happiness level I was at before my accident. Many days I cry and don't know which way is up, because I sit and look at all my major deficits. I know that other students are going to judge me or tease me and it's going to hurt. I just wish that I wore a helmet on that fateful day a year ago!

I want to take the time to say thank you to all of you who have been my support team! My family is amazing! They have given me everything I could ever want or need! Last night we celebrated my "2nd" Birthday... Because, April 22nd is my second chance in life! I lived! I got a beautiful new guitar! It's so pretty and the sound is fantastic!

Sooo thanks everyone who has been there to help me through this really though time! I can't wait to say all the things that I have accomplished at the two-year mark! So here's to YEAR ONE of my recovery... bring on YEAR TWO! Lets see what all I can do! Thanks to all of you who have been a rock for me to lean on! Thanks to those of you who donated money to my cause! Thanks to those of you who have kept me in your prayers! Thanks to those of you who believed in me even at my worst stage! Here's to it!

So, I am at school, studying graphic design at the Art Institute of Indianapolis. I was so excited to get to finally meet some other people, who were around my same age. To be able to step into a school setting and challenge myself, even though I knew I would have to try harder than ever before, I had complete faith in myself. My Mom motivated me so much; sometimes I doubted if I could do it. I asked myself, would people want to befriend me, but, my Mom reminded me how outgoing and loving I have always been. One thing that my brain injury didn't affect was my outgoing and loving personality. I have always been a talker, a person who would talk to a complete stranger whom I came in contact with. My Mom was right, that part of me, was not affected.

While attending the Art Institute of Indianapolis I had the opportunity to re-establish a group of friends. I also had the opportunity to challenge myself, as a person and my disabilities. Now, school was extremely hard. It definitely was not the same as before my accident. However, I was able to get some help through the disabilities support office, they assigned me a few note takers and I was given extra time for assignments and was able to take tests away from other classmates. Some teachers even allowed me to use a notecard, filled with notes, to help prompt me to information.

Some of the challenging moments in school- UGH… I can remember taking a drawing class. I have never been an amazing artist, I can draw, take pictures, and make pottery, but I am no professional artist. I am, what I like to call "so-so". But, I love art. Anyhow, I was taking a drawing and perspective class.

We got to the last assignment, where we had to draw a cityscape, filled with buildings, signs, lights, etc. I still had vision loss at this point; I couldn't see things in 3D. I never realized this before, but I didn't understand it. The teacher that I had, he didn't seem to get it. I would just sit in class and draw whatever was on my mind, I was ignoring the assignment. Trying to push it out of my mind, because I knew I couldn't do it.

I was sitting at home one night, working on other assignments and I started to cry. I was so upset, because this assignment was to be a large portion of my overall grade. GPA was very important to me, because I had something to prove. I needed to see my name on the Dean's List! I needed to show everyone who ever doubted that I would be able to go back to school. I was on a mission. I kept drawing the building blocks and shading. Then, I moved to bigger paper and drew one line at a time, in proper perspective and I started to see buildings. I knew it! I could do it! I sat for 10 hours and didn't let my hand leave the pencil. I ended up drawing a beautiful city, in my mind. But, I didn't get an A on that assignment, I didn't get a B., and in fact I ended up getting a C. I cried and cried, because I felt that the teacher didn't take into consideration that I don't see the world like everyone else can. My vision limits how I see things. I told him, close one of your eyes, I don't care which one and then open the other, but cover half of it with your hand. I said, that's what I see! He didn't cover his eyes, I sometimes wonder if he went home that night and did. But, I will never know.

I hope that in sharing my story I can inspire others who are struggling with a TBI or possibly a caregiver or family member. Nothing is impossible with perseverance and self-dedication to your dreams and goals.

Through my recovery I have met many other people who day in and day out are dealing with the same deficits or worse as mine. I know my TBI has changed my life, but in no way has it ruined it!

6
Adjusting to My Disabilities

Adjusting to my disabilities. Well, I was trying too. I didn't know hardly anyone who was disabled. I knew there were tons of people out there that couldn't walk and stuff like that, but I hadn't met many of them.

I got the amazing opportunity to go to Arizona for a disabled veterans sports camp. It was intended to teach people with disabilities about the sports that we could still play while in a wheelchair. I had no clue that such sports existed. I guess I was under informed. I flew out to Arizona, surrounded by other veterans who were in similar situations as myself. I made tons of friends while I was there!

Sports and disabilities are one! I learned how to play wheelchair tennis, wheelchair basketball; I watched others play wheelchair rugby. It was phenomenal. I had no clue that I could still play sports! I was hooked! I got home and was on a mission to find a way to play wheelchair tennis and other sports in Indiana. I googled it for hours and hours and finally found that the Rehab Hospital of Indianapolis offers sports for people in wheelchairs. I was shocked that I had never heard of the program before, because I did my outpatient therapy through RHI. Anyhow, I got ahold of the program met the coach of the tennis team and I started to play! I attended practices regularly and started to relearn the sport. There is only one difference in regular tennis and wheelchair tennis. People who are playing in a wheelchair get two bounces, instead of the typical one.

It was amazing. I felt like I was normal again, able to play sports and meet more people with disabilities. RHI then offered a water skiing clinic! I have always loved the water. I signed up for the event and had no clue how people could water ski if they couldn't support themselves standing up! Well, ladies and gentleman there are adaptive water skis for people with disabilities. Again, I was amazed! So, I went skiing for the first time since my accident. It was a lovely experience. Being able to float above the water and go over the wake.

Then I was off to Denver, Colorado for the annual Veterans Wheelchair Games! First of all, I was very excited to go to Denver, because my Dad, Kaye, Craig and Shaye live in Denver. So, I signed up to compete in weight lifting, bowling, and air rifles. Now mind you, I was no weight lifter and certainty had never bowled in a wheelchair. I was in for a HUGE shock!

Weightlifting was easy. I bench pressed 150 lb.'s with a slight amount of ease and got awarded the Gold Metal in my weight class! I was ecstatic! Next, it came to bowling. I was so nervous. I sucked at bowling standing up, how was I going to do it, sitting in a wheelchair? I rolled up to my lane and my wheel was in my way. So, I readjusted myself and still it wasn't right. I was extremely close to giving up on bowling when a woman came down to help me. She taught me that I had to sit against my right wheel and push my weight with my left hand over to the right side. With my right hand I had a lot of room to swing the ball straight down the wooden aisle. Needless to say, it was my first time. But, I did great! I won the Gold Metal for bowling! I was on cloud nine!

I met some fabulous people at the games. People who left a mark on my heart, because of their kindness and open hearts! ABC Medical staff was amazing. I am so blessed to be able to say that I met the wonderful owner and founder of the company Tricia LaBar. Tricia won the player of the year award and she absolutely deserved it! She was an inspiration! Next year the games are in Pittsburg, Pennsylvania and I plan on competing for some more gold medals!

7

Blind Rehab at Hines

It was a short plane ride from Indianapolis to Chicago, IL. When I arrived, I was scared. I didn't know what to expect. I wheeled myself to baggage claim and waited for the driver to pick me up. He arrived and we started our journey to the hospital. The VA hospital in Chicago is huge, much larger than the VA hospital in Indianapolis. I was doing my breathing exercises because I was anxious to learn what was going to happen.

The driver was very kind, unloaded my luggage from his van and some of the employees from The Blind Rehab center helped to transport my luggage into my assigned room and then they gave me a tour of the facility. I had a room to myself, which was lovely. However, that is how it typically works at Veterans Hospitals.

Then, I got to meet the staff and other patients. It was a Saturday when I arrived and classes wouldn't take place until Monday morning. So, I had a few days to adjust to my new surroundings. I am extremely social, so I made friends with all of the other veterans and most of the employees who work at Hines VA Medical Center very quickly.

The weekend flew by! On Monday I had an extremely busy day. My schedule was packed for morning till' 5PM. I had Orientation and Mobility, Leatherworking, Woodworking, Manual Skills, and Computer Training. Each class offered different types of training, so that I could better adjust to life as a visually impaired person.

I really enjoyed my woodworking class and loved the opportunity in which I was able to learn braille. I made some gorgeous pieces in my woodworking class, three gorgeous lamps and a candleholder. I would love to continue to make items out of wood, I feel like I learned a skill in which I will continue to use. It was amazing to learn how much you can still do without using your vision. Being able to sand large pieces of wood, just by feeling the texture of the wood.

The whole idea of being sent to blind rehab was so that a person can learn to use their other available senses to continue to live an independent life. The staff and patients at Hines enjoyed me being around, in fact, I was asked to be the Mayor while I was there for treatment. As Mayor I collected money weekly from the other veterans for our coffee fund. I also cooked sweets for the guys a few times a week. Making brownies, cookies, and cakes.

I made so wonderful friends while at Hines. I met men who have no vision and have been to blind rehab plenty of times, they come back to learn new software so that they can continue to live a free life. I am pretty sure I will have to go back to Hines or another type of center that is centered around people suffering from vision loss, at some point, to continue to adapt my life around being visually impaired.

I got extremely depressed while I was at Hines. I had been driving up until the day that I got there. I knew it wasn't a good idea, but I needed my independence. I was in the eye doctor's office when she gave me the news. My heart dropped, she said, "Katie, you can no longer legally drive. I will call the department of motor vehicles in Indianapolis, Indiana and you will have to turn in your license." I started balling my eyes out. I told her that I wanted to see a neuro-ophthalmologist, so that they could make that decision. I wanted to be sure that there was no way I could get my vision back. She agreed.

But, everyday, my depression was getting deeper and deeper. I using a wheelchair about 90% of the time and I told myself, if I can't drive anymore then I am going to walk. At that time, the only feezable way of ever walking again was to have my left leg amputated above the knee. My leg pain was terrible, I had such severe pain everyday, and I thought that was the only option. So, out of complete stupidity I cut the circulation off of my leg. The pain was terrible, but it wasn't much worse than my daily pain. I could do it. I was stronger than that temporary pain, because in my head, I knew that this would damage the blood supply and they would have no choice but to amputate my leg.

Well, I was wrong. Instead of getting my leg amputated, that horrific decision landed me into a psych ward. I was so mad, that I was going to a psych ward. I thought I was "too strong" to go to such a place. I kept telling the staff that I wasn't suicidal, that I was trying to make my life better. Of course, they still assumed I was suicidal and kept me in the psych ward until I agreed to not take my medical issues into my own hands.

Being in the Psych ward gave me time to think. You see, I had never really dealt with my disabilities; instead I would make little jokes about being disabled. I don't think I had taken the time to confront my daily challenges. When your life is thrown around, tossed and turned. You have to stand up and regroup. That's something I hadn't done. It's not like other conditions, where you know you are going to go through a rough patch of life, mine came out of nowhere.

Katie L. Patterson

One day I was a fully functioning person and the next I wasn't even able to care for myself. Taking the time, while in Psych ward to get my anger and frustration out, was probably very beneficial. I didn't realize how much anger I had pent up in my hurt and soul.

8

A Step in the Right Direction

I got home from blind rehab and my family welcomed with open arms and huge hearts. My Mom seemed so mad at me, because I didn't talk openly about my pain. We talked and talked on the drive home and she said she would find away to help me with my pain! I said, Mom, everyone thinks I am okay. I always have a huge smile on my face, but the pain is taking over my life. I got people's attention with that threat. My social worker and parents knew there was something that had to be done. My Mom did some research and found a pain specialist. Luckily, my Medicare had just gone into effect, so I could see a doctor outside of the VA.

I walked in Dr. Ferrell's with my crutches underneath my arms and my wonderful Aunt walking right behind me. I wasn't hoping for a miracle that day and I had no clue what this doctor could do to help me, but it was a step in the right direction. Dr. Ferrell looked at me and said, "I can help you!"

I was shocked. I didn't think anyone could help me get better. I had just put in my mind that I would always be in terrible pain and that would be my life. Because the only thing the Veterans hospital wanted to do, was to put me in a pain group. I didn't want to sit and explain my pain to a bunch of grumpy old men. Talking about pain had not helped me in the past and I sure as heck didn't want to try it again. Because of that decision, the VA said they couldn't do anything. Of course, I could have taken pain pills to block the pain, but I refused to take them or even fill them when ordered by previous doctors. I didn't want my pain to make me an addict. Which I honestly think is what made people presume that I was fine. If I was in such horrific pain everyday, then I would have asked for pain pills. I didn't want that. I didn't want to take a pill every 6 hours to help me function. That wasn't me and I refused to manage my pain in that way.

A few days later, I was in the operating room. That wonderful doctor implanted a trial version of a spinal cord stimulator. To get approval from any insurance company for the permanent spinal cord stimulator, the patient has to try the trial version first to see if it helps with their pain. That day, after the surgery, I woke up and was pain free in my legs. I went from having severe pain that put me in tears everyday to being pretty much pain free. I had no clue what to think!

In my head, I thought, this has to be a dream. There isn't anyway possible that my pain is primarily gone. But, it was and I was so sad the next week when I had to go in and have the temporary one removed. I cried the night before, telling myself, I don't want the pain back. It was a week of heaven with very little pain. But, I had to have it removed, so that I could have the permanent one implanted in my back.

Having it removed made me so sad and they weren't sure how long it would take to get approval from Medicare to have the permanent devise implanted in my back. But, the next day I received a phone call to schedule the surgery! I was elated! I knew there would be an end to my pain.

I was in the operating room, preparing to be put to sleep when the doctor told me she would wake me up during surgery, so she could put the electronic stimulators in the correct place. I don't remember getting woken up during surgery, but she placed it in the perfect spot! This time I did have pain after surgery, but that was due to the rather large incisions. It took a 4-inch incision down my spine and a 4-inch incision on my hip to implant the devise. But, I knew I could handle postoperative pain! That was nothing in comparison to what I used to deal with everyday!

I am on the road to recovery now. I don't wake up crying in the night now. I can be more mobile without the fear of pain. I do still have major leg issues and I will for the rest of my life. There is no way I will ever be able to be a runner or play regular tennis. But, I can walk again. Each step I take is hard, because I lost so much muscle being confined to a wheelchair for two and a half years.

I know and the doctors have said I will need a knee replacement, because I have the legs of an 80-year-old woman. However, currently medical science isn't able to provide a knee replacement that will last long enough. So, I will wait. I know that I am on the road to recovery. I know that I can be the woman that I was meant to be!

My heart goes out to people who are experiencing chronic pain, it is exhausting. Pain can drain you and it also can change you. You can't let pain rule your life, as it becomes a full time job. I was allowing my pain to control every aspect of my life. I wasn't going out with friends or family, I was becoming a recluse. For anyone who knows me, they know that, that is not who I am. I have always been someone who wants to be out and about meeting people and staying physically active.

9
What is a TBI?

A TBI is a traumatic brain injury. TBI's are any type of head trauma from concussions to contusions. Thousands and thousands of people every year suffer from such trauma. Brain injuries are scary, because people don't know much about them. I had no clue, even as a nursing student how fragile the brain is. I know now, what I wish I could have known then.

In most other aspects, a traumatic brain injury is very different. Since our brain defines who we are, the consequences of a brain injury can affect all aspects of our lives, including our personality. A brain injury is different from a broken limb or punctured lung. An injury in these areas limit the use of a specific part of your body, but your personality and mental abilities remain unchanged. Most often, these body structures heal and regain their previous function.

Brain injuries do not heal like other injuries. Recovery is a functional recovery, based on mechanisms that remain uncertain. No two-brain injuries are alike and the consequence of two similar injuries may be very different. Symptoms may appear right away or may not be present for days or weeks after the injury.

One of the consequences of brain injury is that the person often does not realize that a brain injury has occurred.

How many people have TBI?

TBIs contribute to a substantial number of deaths and cases of permanent disability annually.

Of the 1.4 million who sustain a TBI each year in the United States: 50,000 die; 235,000 are hospitalized; and 1.1 million are treated and released from an emergency department.

Among children ages 0 to 14 years, TBI results in an estimated:
2,685 deaths;
37,000 hospitalizations; and
435,000 emergency department visits annually.
The number of people with TBI who are not seen in an emergency department or who receive no care is unknown.

What causes TBI?
The leading causes of TBI are: Falls (28%);
Motor vehicle-traffic crashes (20%);\
Struck by/against events (19%); and
Assaults (11%).
For more information on the leading causes of TBI, see Causes.

What are the signs and symptoms of TBI?

The signs and symptoms of a traumatic brain injury (TBI) can be subtle. Symptoms of a TBI may not appear until days or weeks following the injury or may even be missed, as people may look fine even though they may act or feel differently.

What are the long-term outcomes of TBI?

CDC estimates that at least 5.3 million Americans, approximately 2% of the U.S. population, currently have a long-term or lifelong need for help to perform activities of daily living as a result of a TBI.

TBI can cause a wide range of functional changes affecting thinking, sensation, language, and/or emotions. It can also cause epilepsy and increase the risk for conditions such as Alzheimer's disease, Parkinson's disease, and other brain disorders that become more prevalent with age.

Brain Anatomy

The brain is the hub of the central nervous system and controls all bodily functions and processes. It weighs about three pounds and is surrounded by protective bone called the skull or cranium. The brain has the texture of gelatin and is held together by three layers of membranes called the dura, pia, and arachnoid.

Between the pia and arachnoid membranes is the subarachnoid space, through which a network of arteries and veins carries blood to and from the heart. Injury to these blood vessels can lead to blood clots, which can exert damaging pressure against the brain's delicate tissue. The brain is surrounded by a cushioning reservoir of cerebrospinal fluid (CSF).

The lower part of the brain (called the brain stem) passes through a hole at the base of the skull and merges with the spinal cord and the rest of the nervous system. The brain stem can be compared to a telephone cable with thousands of individual wires (nerve fibers) that carry signals to and from all parts of the body. The brain stem also regulates such body functions as consciousness, fatigue, heart rate, and blood pressure. Damage to the stem can cause loss of consciousness, or concussion of the brain.

Behind the brain stem is the cerebellum, a curved mass of nerve tissues that regulates balance and coordinates fine motor skills. It enables us to move quickly and smoothly, thread a needle, or throw a dart with accuracy.

The cerebral cortex is the largest part of the brain and is shaped like a large, wrinkled, walnut divided in half (the right and left cerebral hemispheres) and joined at the center. The right hemisphere controls the left side of the body; the left hemisphere controls the right side. In most people, the left hemisphere regulates language and speech and the right hemisphere controls nonverbal, spatial skills such as the ability to draw or play music. If the right side of the brain is damaged, movement in the left arm and leg, vision to the left, or hearing in the left ear, may be affected. An injury to the left side of the brain affects speech and movement on the right side of the body.

The cerebral cortex is further divided into several areas called lobes. Of these:

The left and right frontal lobes, located behind the forehead, control intellectual activities, such as the ability to organize, and figure prominently in personality, behavior, and emotional control.

The temporal lobes, situated immediately behind and below the frontal lobes and just behind the ears, control memory, speech and comprehension.

The parietal lobes located at the back of the head and above the ears, control the ability to read, write, and understand spatial relationships.

The areas between the frontal and parietal lobes regulate movement and sensation.

The occipital lobes, situated at the back of the head, control sight.

In the middle of the cerebral cortex are several small white nuclei, or nerve centers, called the diencephalon. Among these is the pea-sized hypothalamus, which regulates appetite, thirst, temperature, and some aspects of memory and controls sexual arousal. Another is the limbic system, which is associated with the control of emotions and moods.

Damage to these areas can result in impairment to the functions they regulate.

Causes for TBI:

The three most common causes of TBI are the following:

Motor vehicle, bicycle, or vehicle-pedestrian mishaps (more than 50%)
Falls (approximately 25%)
Violence (nearly 20%)
Vehicle-related injuries involve people of all ages. Falls are most common among the elderly and the very young. Alcohol and medication use are common contributing factors in falls. Gunshot wounds account for a small proportion of TBIs (10%), but a high percentage of related fatalities (44%). Nine out of ten people who incur TBI from a firearm die.

Domestic abuse (including shaken baby syndrome) and sports injuries are common causes of TBI. Approximately 3% of all hospitalizations for TBI are incurred while playing sports. Most sports-related TBI are relatively minor and therefore go unreported.

Prognosis

Physicians look at several indicators to predict the level of a patient's recovery during the first few weeks and months after injury:

Duration of coma

Severity of coma in the first few hours after the injury (as measured by the Glasgow Coma Score)
Duration of post-traumatic amnesia (PTA)
Location and size of contusions and hemorrhages in the brain
Severity of injuries to other body systems sustained at the time of the TBI

Precise predictions are difficult with TBI, but some generalizations can be made:

The more severe the injury, the longer the recovery period, and the more impairment a survivor will have once recovery has plateaued.
Recovery from diffuse axonal injury takes longer than recovery from focal contusions.
Recovery from TBI with hypoxic injury is less complete than without significant hypoxic injury.

The need for surgery does not necessarily indicate a worse outcome. For example, a patient requiring the removal of a blood clot may recover as completely as one who never needs surgery.

Specific areas of the brain control cognitive and behavioral processes, so the location of the injury determines the type of impairment. For example, patients who suffer a diffuse axonal injury and/or a diffuse hypoxic injury often have difficulty with concentration and long-term memory. They may have trouble dealing with more than one thing at a time, difficulty keeping track of appointments, and keeping organized. Those who suffer focal contusions or hemorrhages have problems associated with the particular brain areas affected. For example, a hemorrhage deep in the left side of the brain may cause weakness of the right side of the body. A patient with contusions of the frontal lobes may have trouble being organized or may have behavioral problems such as abnormal passivity, impulsiveness, or aggressiveness.

The length of time a patient spends in a coma correlates to both post-traumatic amnesia (PTA) and recovery times:

Coma lasting seconds to minutes results in PTA that lasts hours to days; recovery plateau occurs over days to weeks.

Coma that lasts hours to days results in PTA lasting days to weeks; recovery plateau occurs over months.

Coma lasting weeks results in PTA that lasts months; recovery plateau occurs over months to years.

Physicians trained in the care of brain-injured patients can best determine how these generalizations apply to a particular TBI survivor.

There are several mechanisms of recovery after brain injury. Initial improvement may be due to the reduction of swelling (edema) of brain tissue occurring over days, weeks or months, depending on the severity of the injury. Next, damaged brain cells begin functioning again, usually over a period weeks to months. Finally, undamaged areas of the brain may, to a certain extent, take over the functions of areas that suffer permanent damage.

I urge parents to teach their children the importance of helmets. I didn't have a helmet on, on that fateful day. Helmets are so important. Our brains are so fragile. The brain is a scary organ. Once brain tissue is damaged, there is no way for it to regrow. It isn't like our skin that can get a scab and then heal. Our brain can, however, it can grow new connections, but that doesn't always happen.

I wish I could turn back time and tell myself then, what I know now. But, again, that will never happen. Had I had a helmet on, I would have still had a concussion, but my brain injury would have not been as severe as it was.

What did my brain injury damage? Well, my major damage was done to my frontal lobe, temporal lobe, and occipital lobe. The frontal lobe damage caused damage to my short-term memory. Which is sometimes extremely frustrating! Speech therapy taught me methods to work with to adjust to my memory loss. I sometimes feel like I have notes and calendar everywhere. The damage to my occipital lobe has been the most frustrating. The occipital lobe controls your vision. Mine was severely injured and to this day continues to get worse. If I get a migraine, that will allow my brain to swell due to the pressure. That will then place pressure on the occipital nerve, which continues to make my vision worse.

Brain injuries are becoming increasingly common. It is the signature injury for the OIF OEF Veterans who are fighting for our country. Since my injury I have met tons of people who suffer from TBI's as well. I have met many other veterans who suffer from the effects of a TBI. Some brain injuries are worse than others! Had I hit the left side of my head during the accident, I would have lost all memory of my previous life and abilities. The left side of your brain holds your long-term memories. Often times, people who suffer from left side brain injuries have to relearn everything. I am extremely lucky that I didn't have damage to that lobe.

What else did I loose from my traumatic brain injury? Obviously as mentioned previously I lost a lot of my vision, I also lost all of my hearing in my right ear. Due to the injury I lost the ability to taste and smell. Which has been very interesting. I have taught myself to eat for texture. It's working thus far. Maybe one day I will come out with a cookbook!

Why do I call it the invisible injury? It's extremely frustrating, because I know that I have major disabilities. But, if you look at me, I look fine. I don't have any scars on my face and I don't walk around with an eye patch on. People have no clue that I am disabled.

So when I have people knocking on the window of my car and screaming at me telling me, to move my car because I am not disabled. They assume because of my age, there is no way that she can be disabled. It is so frustrating. My disability is no different from anyone else's disability and my age shouldn't matter. I have learned to roll my eyes and go about my day, without letting it get to me.

I urge you, tell your children, grandchildren, nieces and nephews to always wear a helmet when riding a bike, skateboard, or rollerblades. Our brains are so extremely precious! Don't loose what you can't ever gain back.

10
What's Next in My Life?

My goals and aspirations are set so very high for myself. I want to graduate college with honors and due to my disabilities I get extended time, which really helps me out! I am going to get my undergraduate degree in Registered Nursing. I have changed my major several times since my accident. I was told that I couldn't be a nurse. But, I am not going to let a doctor decide what I can and cannot be. Being a nurse is something I have always wanted to do and I feel it is still a mission I can accomplish.

I was going to school for Graphic design, but due to my vision loss there was no way that I could stare at a computer screen for 8 hours a day without is negatively affecting what vision I have left. Then, I changed my major to Psychology, but I decided that I didn't want to be in school for another 6ish years. Because, you can't do much with a bachelor in psychology, you have to get a graduate degree and sometimes even a doctorate.

I also want to be a homeowner again some day; I lost mine due to foreclosure after my accident. I want to have a home that I can invite friends and family over and share laughter and love with. I want to be able to push a lawn mower through the grass and know that I can do it.

I want to be a wife and a mother. I feel that I will be an incredible mother; the best mother in the world taught me. She is my rock and my foundation, without her I wouldn't be the woman I am today. She is my biggest cheerleader and best friend.

I want to teach people who have suffered from a TBI, that there is life at the end of such a terrible accident. I want to fly across the nation from hospital to hospital to meet other survivors and learn their stories. There are so many people in the world who have suffered an injury very similar or worse than mine. I want to get to know them, inspire them to keep on fighting. I feel like, meeting someone who has survived a similar battle to one that you are fighting is instrumental in healing, to see a light at the end of a very dark tunnel. I remember meeting an Army Veteran who was severely injured while deployed to Iraq. I was lying in the same room, where he did part of his rehab. Koko was that light for me and my family. Our injuries were extremely different, but we both were survivors from traumatic brain injuries. I saw hope in his eyes and knew that healing was possible.

I flew to New York last year and shot a pilot cooking show called, "The Tasteless Chef." It was a show that was going to teach people who lacked the ability to taste and smell, how to still enjoy cooking. The pilot went well, I was extremely nervous. I suppose one day I could still get offered a show, but for now I am a daughter, partner, friend, and sister.

I feel that God is a powerful and loving God. I will never know why I got hurt on the sunny April day in 2008. But, God has something bigger and greater planned for me. One day, I will know what that is. For now, I will continue to be his soldier and spread his word with my open and loving heart!

11
It's Been 3 Years

I have learned so much in the past three years. I have learned how to readjust my whole entire life. I have had many surgeries and am still scheduled to have more. I wish that people understood brain injuries more. I can only hope, that with the growing numbers of these injuries, people will begin to learn. When I tell people that I have a brain injury, they don't know what that means. I am in no way retarted; I am a little bit slower. But, I have amazing potential. I refuse to let my disability control my life.

On April 22nd of 2011, it will have been three years. Some days I find myself being negative to myself, thinking that things will never get better. But, I have the strength of my family and friends. I have wanted to throw in the towel and stop trying, so many times. But, that doesn't get you anywhere. I have learned that my patience is not what it should be. I have also learned that I get angry more easily and I put myself down a lot. I always find myself not allowing myself to hear my own excuses. It's Ohhhh my back hurts, my legs, hurt, I am tired, or I have a migraine. But, I have stopped allowing myself to do that.

I realize that I do have to take breaks; I have to allow myself to heal. But, I am afraid that if I take a long break, then I will quit trying. I can't burry myself in my misery any longer.

I never thought that life would be this hard. I had a great family and a good head on my shoulders. I was the girl that would go far. The one who refused to quit. Even when challenges got thrown into my path, I kept finding a way to the top.

12
Thank You

I want to take a moment to say thank you to a few people!

Mom,

You have been my rock and my foundation! Without you stepping in to get me the medical treatment I needed, I would be lost. You have encouraged me to never give up and to continue to work towards my goals and ambitions! You are my mentour and best friend, I feel so blessed to have you as my Mom!

Dad,

Thank you for being there when I got hurt, I know it was tough seeing your baby girl as sick as I was, but you stood strong! I love you Papa Smurf!

Megan,

Thank you for being there to support Mom when I was at my worst! Thank you for taking time from your busy schedule to be by my bedside to hold my hand! I am so happy you had the opportunity to travel, once my health was stable! Never stop living your dreams my lil' world traveler!

Craig,

Thank you for starting the blog for our family and friends, to keep everyone up to date on my struggles and recovery! Also, thank you for being by Mom and my side, during some of the most scary weeks. I love you!

Aunt Bonnie,

Thank you for putting your life on hold to come and hold my Mom's hand through the whole entire process. Without you there she would have broken down. I appreciate you stopping your life, to come and save another!

Lauren & Ashley,

Thank you so much for starting a "Kause" in my name! That allowed money to be raised to get me from Richmond, VA to Indianapolis, IN. Without your help, the process would have taken more time! The Walk/Run was such a success!

To the Rest of My Family,

I promise, I didn't forget about any of you! Thank you all of your prayers, thoughts, and monies!

To the PolyTrauma Ritz Unit at the Indianapolis, IN VA Medical Center, Robbie, Dr. Mosier, Tashia, Sandi, Alex and others,

Thank you so much for making room for me in your unit so that I could be back in Indiana. All of you and everyone else who I forgot to mention played a vital part in my recovery and I am forever grateful!

To the RHI Staff in Indianapolis, Indiana

Dr. Thank you for continuing to work with me in my recovery! Your staff was extremely welcoming and understanding of my injuries!

To the Hines VA Blind Rehab Staff:

Thank you so much for teaching me how to adapt my life around my vision loss. I had a wonderful time in woodworking, leather working, orientation and mobility, computer training, and learning braille! Thank you!

To Dr. Ferrell and Staff:

Thank you for allowing me to get out of pain! Without you I would still be in severe pain daily! You are an amazing doctor and I appreciate your ability to help with patients suffering from severe nerve pain! You ROCK!!!

To Advanced Physical Therapy:
Tami and Cheryl

Ladies you are amazing Physical therapists and therapy assistants! I loved working with both of you and I couldn't have worked with a better group of woman! I hope your other patients listen to you when you tell them to "slow down"!

Do you have disabilities and are interested in learning more about wheelchair athletics?

Please make sure you do some research and find a team in your home state! I say to you, don't let your disabilities stop you! They stopped me for so long!

Do you have a brain injury and need support in dealing with your disabilities?

Please, find a support center! I know Indianapolis offers them through the Rehab Hospital of Indianapolis!

Are you Blind, going Blind, or have vision loss?

Please, talk to Hadley School for the Blind. They will offer you resources to further your education and offer methods of learning to meet the disability of the student.
http://www.hadley.edu

Also, apply for a service dog! Service dogs are amazing. My service dog is in training right now! I can't wait until he finishes training and can become a vital part of my daily life!

Depressed?

I have been there and I can't say that I still don't get depressed, because I do. Sometimes life is hard and believe me, I get it!

Please seek help! It is out there!

National Suicide Prevention Hotline!!!

Are you in crisis?
Please call 1-800-273-TALK

Are you a veteran in emotional distress? Please call
1-800-273-TALK and
Press 1 to be routed to the Veterans Suicide Prevention Hotline

For Hearing and Speech Impaired with TTY Equipment:
1-800-799-4TTY (4889)